Hey, Bestie

(THIS IS WHY I LOVE YA)

DON'T FREAK OUT,

BUT YOU'RE MY #1...

- WORK
- SCHOOL
- TRAVEL
- LIFELONG
- INSTANT
- EVERYDAY
- NEW
-

...BESTIE.

ARE WHAT LIFE'S ALL ABOUT.

WE ALL NEED KINDRED PALS TO RUN ALONGSIDE US—TO HIGH-FIVE WHEN WE SUCCEED AND TO TOAST TO ANOTHER TRY WHEN WE DON'T.

LIFE IS MADE RICHER BY BESTIES LIKE YOU, WHO LEAP INTO THE UNKNOWN WITH ME, YELLING AS WE FLY, HOLDING HANDS.

TOGETHER,
WE COULD CONQUER
ANYTHING.

Besties like you

OUR FRIENDSHIP IS A
WARM MUG OF MEMORIES
WAITING TO BE
MADE—AND THAT
KIND OF CONNECTION
DOESN'T COOL.

BUT THE THING IS,
IT DOESN'T MATTER
WHAT WE DO OR
HOW OFTEN WE SEE
EACH OTHER.

AT THE VERY LEAST,
I HOPE WE CAN

____

____

MORE.

IF IT WERE UP TO ME,
WE'D DROP EVERYTHING AND

____

____

TOGETHER.

EVEN IF WE HAVEN'T CHATTED IN AGES, WE ALWAYS FALL RIGHT BACK INTO THE GOOD STUFF.

LIKE A HOT COCOA AFTER A SNOWBALL FIGHT, YOU BRING COLOR AND WARMTH BACK INTO MY DAMP LITTLE HEART.

AND calm TO MY
CHAOS.

YOU ADD SPARKLE TO
DREARY DAYS,

FiLL
My
CUP

Besties
like
you

IF WE TURN OUT TO BE THE LAST CREATURES OF OUR KIND, WE'LL SCRAWL OUR STORIES ON CAVE WALLS TO SHOW THE FUTURE WORLD WHAT FRIENDSHIP REALLY LOOKED LIKE.

BESTIES

HOW ELSE TO EXPLAIN OUR SHARED OBSESSION WITH

______________?

IT'S LIKE YOU AND I ARE THE SAME RARE SPECIES AND WE SOMEHOW FOUND EACH OTHER IN THE WILD.

NOW WE'RE OUT HERE, RUNNING OUR OWN ANIMAL KINGDOM TOGETHER.

YOU MATCH MY MOOD,

AND YOU SHARE MY VIBE.

YOU GET MY JOKES,

AND YOU GET MY WORRIES.

GET IT.

Besties like you

JUST LIKE THAT, YOU BLEW THE DARK CLOUDS AWAY AND LET ME SEE THE SKY.

REMEMBER WHEN I

AND YOU

?

YOU'RE ALREADY THERE WITH MEGAPHONES A-BLASTING, LIFEBOATS AT THE READY, AND A YEAR'S SUPPLY OF SPARKLING DRINKS TO HELP ME FORGET ABOUT THE STORM.

I DON'T EVEN HAVE TO FIRE THE FLARE GUN.

YOU CAN TELL WHEN THINGS ARE GOING SIDEWAYS AND MY SHIP IS TAKING ON WATER.

SAVE
THE
DAY.

Besties
like
you

WITH YOU, THERE'S
NO PERFORMANCE.
NO STAGE, NO
LIGHTING, NO
LAUGH TRACK.

INSTEAD, IT'S JUST
THE TWO OF US,
SNEAKING TREATS
TOGETHER BACKSTAGE.

ONCE I DISCOVERED...

- HOW HILARIOUS YOU ARE
- HOW INCREDIBLY KIND YOU ARE
- HOW WE'RE ALMOST THE SAME PERSON
- YOU LOVE THE SAME THINGS I LOVE
- YOU ACTUALLY ARE MADE OUT OF PIXIE DUST AND SPRINKLES

...I KNEW WE'D BE BESTIES.

WHEN I FIRST MET YOU, I THOUGHT:

- ☐ "WOW, THIS PERSON IS COOL."
- ☐ "YAY, NEW FRIEND!"
- ☐ "NOW HERE'S SOMEONE I COULD RULE THE WORLD WITH."
- ☐ "WHERE HAVE YOU BEEN ALL MY LIFE?"
- ☐ "THIS PERSON MUST BE MADE OF PIXIE DUST AND SPRINKLES."

YOU KNOW THE SOFT AND QUIRKY UNDERBELLY OF MY PERSONALITY— THE AUTHENTIC LITTLE BITS OF MYSELF I SHARE ONLY IN THE PRESENCE OF TRUE PALS.

YOU KNOW MY
EMBARRASSING TALES AND
MY FAVORITE SNACKS.

KNOW
THINGS.

Besties like you

YOU'RE THE MAPLE SYRUP
TO MY PANCAKES,

AND THE BANANA
TO MY BREAD.

WITHOUT YOU, LIFE WOULD
BE A LOT LESS SWEET.

WHEN I NEED:

YOU ALWAYS:

TO:
YOU!

YOU'RE THERE WHEN I NEED YOU,
BECAUSE YOU HAVE A GOLDEN HEART
AND A SUGAR-FROSTED SOUL,

AND BECAUSE YOU KNOW
I'D DO THE EXACT SAME THING
FOR YOU, IF GIVEN A CHANCE.

YOU CAN'T HELP IT.
YOU SHOW UP BECAUSE
YOU CARE AND BECAUSE YOU'RE
JUST SO DANG WONDERFUL.

SHOW UP.

Besties like you

I KNOW WHAT YOU'RE THINKING.

"BESTIE? WHAT'S A BESTIE?"

-NEWS FLASH-

YOU ARE!

HOW DO I KNOW?

EVEN...

- ☐ FULL INBOXES
- ☐ A MARSHMALLOW AVALANCHE
- ☐ A HERD OF STAMPEDING GIRAFFES
- ☐ A THOUSAND LOADS OF LAUNDRY
- ☐ HIGH SCHOOL (again)
- ☐ NO WI-FI

Because...
I've got you, Bestie.

AND you've GOT ME.

COMPENDIUM
live inspired

Written by: Danielle Leduc McQueen
Illustrated by: Kim Sielbeck
Edited by: Amelia Riedler
Art Directed by: Justine Edge

Library of Congress Control Number: 2024937148 | ISBN: 978-1-957891-56-9

1st printing. Printed in China with soy inks on FSC®-Mix certified paper.

Create meaningful moments with gifts that inspire.

CONNECT WITH US
live-inspired.com | sayhello@compendiuminc.com

@compendiumliveinspired
#compendiumliveinspired